This Journal Belongs To

How Do I Feel?

A Mental Health Journal for Kids

Becca Heiden, PhD

ROCKRIDGE
PRESS

To my parents and Brendan:
Thank you for your endless support.

Contents

Welcome to Your Journal

Welcome to your very own mental health journal! My name is Dr. Becca, and I am a psychologist who works with kids just like you. When I was your age, I found it very helpful to write down my thoughts and ideas. I decided to make this journal to help guide you to do the same thing.

This book is *all* for you! It is designed to help you be the *best* that you can be. Your journal will help you think about your emotions, thoughts, relationships, behaviors, and many other things. It is a space to check in with yourself, learn, grow, and express who you are.

Remember: All emotions are okay, and we all feel lots of different things. It's okay not to feel happy all the time. This journal will help you learn how to deal with all kinds of feelings. You'll also find out ways to make difficult things a little bit easier.

What Is Mental Health?

Mental health is our well-being, or how we are doing in life. It refers to our heart, our brain, and our relationships with others. It affects what we feel and what we think about every day. And it is just as important as your physical health!

What does it look like to be mentally healthy? It often looks like having a lot of emotions, such as happiness, joy, and excitement. You also have good thoughts, like being proud of yourself and being confident. When you're mentally healthy, you are able to deal with your emotions, even tough ones like anger and sadness.

There are three parts of mental health: emotional health, psychological health, and social health. Emotional health has to do with your heart and your emotions. It is your ability to manage all your emotions. Psychological health has more to do with your brain and your thoughts. It is your ability to think in helpful ways, solve problems, and remember things you can do to cope. Finally, social health is all about relationships, like those with family and friends. The people in your life affect your mental health, so it's important to build positive relationships whenever you can.

Mental Health Tips

Here are six tips to keep yourself mentally healthy!

1. **Check in on your basic needs.** Make sure you are getting enough sleep, eating healthy, and drinking lots of water.

2. **Follow routines.** Having a routine that you follow can make life easier. For example, doing your homework right after school can open up more time for fun activities before dinner.

3. **Make time for self-care activities.** Self-care activities help you feel like you are taking care of yourself. Playing with friends, petting your dog or cat, taking a bubble bath, and going on a walk are all good examples!

4. **Talk openly about your feelings.** Sometimes we want to hide our emotions away. But sharing them helps us understand them and deal with them. Practice opening up with someone you feel close to and comfortable around.

5. **Stay active.** Getting your body moving is really helpful for your mental and physical health. Remember to stay active throughout the week.

6. **Ask for help.** When you feel like you need help, do not be afraid to ask for it! Talk to your teachers, parents, grandparents, or other close relatives. They are great sources of support.

How to Use This Journal

This journal is a place for you to write, draw, and reflect. Many pages will give you a prompt that encourages you to think about things. You can then write your thoughts down on paper. Other pages will give you an activity to try out. There are also tips and strategies for you to practice in everyday life.

Many kids will start on the first page of this journal and work through the book page by page. Some kids might progress in random order based on the pages they find most helpful. I recommend you start at the beginning and complete your journal page by page, but it is up to you. This is your journey!

Your journal will hopefully be very helpful, but it's okay if you find yourself struggling. If you feel like you need more help, talk to a parent, guardian, or counselor. Sometimes people need more than just a journal to become mentally healthy and feel better.

Now turn the page to get started on your mental health journey!

PART 1

Heart Space

Emotional mental health is our ability to understand what we feel and to cope with the emotions we experience. This section will increase your awareness of your feelings. You will also learn ways to control your feelings. The prompts and activities will help you become more connected to your heart space, or your inner self.

DATE: _____

TODAY'S MOOD: 🙂 😀 😧 😐 😠

The first step to understanding your emotions is to put a name to them. Having a strong emotional vocabulary is very helpful. What are all the emotions and feelings you can think of?

_____

_____

_____

_____

_____

_____

_____

_____

_____

_____

_____

_____

_____

DATE: _____

TODAY'S MOOD: ☺ 😀 ☹ 😐 😠

Take some time to think of the six to eight emotions
that you feel most often. What are the names of these
emotions? When have you felt these emotions in
your life?

_____

_____

_____

_____

_____

_____

_____

_____

_____

_____

_____

_____

_____

DATE: _____

TODAY'S MOOD: 🙂 😀 ☹️ 😐 😠

Did you know emotions express themselves in our bodies? When you feel anxious, for example, your heart might start racing or you might get a stomachache. Think of the different emotions you experience. Where do you feel them in your body?

_____

_____

_____

_____

_____

_____

_____

_____

_____

_____

_____

_____

DATE: _____

TODAY'S MOOD:

A Mindful Moment

One of the most helpful ways to connect with your emotions is to pause and focus on your breath. This breathing exercise is something that you can do anywhere. All you need is your hands!

First, put your left hand out in front of you and spread your fingers apart. Take your right index finger and place it on your left wrist. Slowly begin to trace the outside of your thumb. Breathe in deeply as you slide your finger up the thumb. Continue down the inside of your thumb as you slowly breathe out. Repeat this process of tracing and breathing until you reach your pinky finger.

After you finish this activity, check in with yourself. Is your breathing slower and calmer? Do your emotions feel more under control? Deep breathing helps us relax our bodies and calm our minds.

DATE: _____

TODAY'S MOOD: ☺ 😄 ☹ 😐 😠

Some emotions make you feel good. Others make you feel not so good. What are some emotions that make you feel good inside?

_____

_____

_____

_____

_____

_____

_____

_____

_____

_____

_____

_____

_____

_____

DATE: _____

TODAY'S MOOD: ☺ 😀 ☹ 😐 😠

Being proud of yourself can make you feel good!
When was a time in your life you felt very proud of
yourself or proud of something you accomplished?

_____

_____

_____

_____

_____

_____

_____

_____

_____

_____

_____

_____

_____

_____

DATE: _____

TODAY'S MOOD:

Challenge Yourself!

One way to increase feel-good emotions is by trying something you have never done before. Take a few minutes to think of something fun you have not tried yet. It could be anything, like roller-skating or painting a picture. Put your plans into action and give it a try! How did you feel after trying something new? Did your positive emotions increase?

_____

_____

_____

_____

_____

_____

_____

_____

_____

DATE: _____

TODAY'S MOOD: ☺ 😀 ☹ 😐 😣

Some emotions don't make us feel good. These
are emotions that lead to frustration and unhelpful
thoughts. What difficult emotions do you experience?
When have your emotions led to negative outcomes?

_____

_____

_____

_____

_____

_____

_____

_____

_____

_____

_____

_____

_____

DATE: _____

TODAY'S MOOD: 😊 😃 ☹️ 😐 😠

One difficult experience everyone has is stress.
Stress is when you feel unable to cope with what is
happening. It can feel overwhelming and frustrating.
What does stress feel like in your body?

_____

_____

_____

_____

_____

_____

_____

_____

_____

_____

_____

_____

_____

_____

DATE: _____

TODAY'S MOOD: ☺ 😀 ☹ 😐 😠

Anger is a difficult emotion. How do you react to anger? Where do you feel it in your body? What types of situations make you lose your temper?

_____

_____

_____

_____

_____

_____

_____

_____

_____

_____

_____

_____

_____

_____

_____

_____

DATE: _____

TODAY'S MOOD: ☺ 😀 ☹ 😐 😠

When we lose our temper, we often act impulsively.
That means we suddenly yell, throw a fit, or in other
ways act without thinking. How does your anger come
out in negative ways? How can you deal with your
anger in more helpful and appropriate ways?

_____

_____

_____

_____

_____

_____

_____

_____

_____

_____

_____

_____

DATE: _____

TODAY'S MOOD: 🙂 😀 🙁 😐 😠

Coping skills are things we can do when we feel stressed or overwhelmed. What do you do that makes you feel happy? How could that activity help you cope in difficult times?

_____

_____

_____

_____

_____

_____

_____

_____

_____

_____

_____

_____

_____

_____

DATE: _____

TODAY'S MOOD: ☺ 😀 ☹ 😐 😠

Look over this list of coping skills, and check off the ones you think might be helpful for you!

- ☐ Count to ten
- ☐ Take a walk
- ☐ Listen to music
- ☐ Take a deep breath
- ☐ Talk to an adult you trust
- ☐ Journal
- ☐ Create something
- ☐ Watch a video or show
- ☐ Sleep
- ☐ Color or draw
- ☐ Take a bath or shower
- ☐ Sing or dance
- ☐ Play outside
- ☐ Ask for help
- ☐ Do a puzzle
- ☐ Play a game
- ☐ Meditate

DATE: _____

TODAY'S MOOD: ☺ 😃 ☹ 😐 😠

Write down five to six situations where difficult emotions have gotten in your way. What happened? What did you feel? How did those difficult emotions make you act?

_____

_____

_____

_____

_____

_____

_____

_____

_____

_____

_____

_____

_____

DATE: _____

TODAY'S MOOD: ☺ 😃 ☹ 😐 😠

Think of a time when difficult emotions made you act impulsively. Do you wish you had acted differently? What coping skills could you have used in this situation?

_____

_____

_____

_____

_____

_____

_____

_____

_____

_____

_____

_____

_____

A Mindful Moment

When we do not manage difficult emotions, we can take negative actions. Now you can learn to STOP yourself before your emotions get out of control.

S = Stop!

The first step is to STOP in your tracks when you feel a difficult emotion coming on. Pausing helps you take a step back and think before acting.

T = Take a breath

Next, take a few long, slow, deep breaths. Breathing helps keep you calm and in control.

O = Observe your emotions

Now that you are feeling more calm, think about what you are feeling and label that emotion.

P = Proceed mindfully

The final step is to proceed in the best way possible to avoid negative consequences. Now that you have recognized your emotion, you can find a way to move forward.

DATE: _____

TODAY'S MOOD: ☺ 😃 ☹ 😐 😠

Reflect on the journaling you have done so far. What has been your favorite prompt or activity? Do you feel more connected with your emotions? What are you hoping to learn next?

_____

_____

_____

_____

_____

_____

_____

_____

_____

_____

_____

_____

_____

DATE: _____

TODAY'S MOOD: ☺ 😀 ☹ 😐 😠

Some feelings make you feel down in the dumps.
These feelings might include sadness, disappointment,
and grief. When in your life have you felt this way?
Where do you feel these emotions in your body?

_____

_____

_____

_____

_____

_____

_____

_____

_____

_____

_____

_____

_____

DATE: _____

TODAY'S MOOD:

A Mindful Moment

Guided imagery is a technique that can help you feel calm. When you use guided imagery, you imagine a peaceful situation, like floating down a river or being up in the clouds. As you picture this situation in your head, you pretend it is happening. Follow the script below to get started!

You are standing in a peaceful meadow. All around you is long grass, swaying in the wind. To your right, there is a field of flowers. There are yellow, pink, and orange ones. A small family of bunnies hops through the grass in front of you. They look so soft and cuddly. To your left, there is a river. You can hear the water flowing downstream. You lie down in the grass, take a deep breath in, and smell the flowers.

Now close your eyes and imagine this scene!

DATE: _____

TODAY'S MOOD: ☺ 😃 ☹ 😐 😠

When you feel down, getting help from loved ones is a great idea. You might want to talk to close friends and trusted adults, like your caregivers or teachers. Who are people in your life you could ask for help?

_____

_____

_____

_____

_____

_____

_____

_____

_____

_____

_____

_____

_____

DATE: _____

TODAY'S MOOD:

A happy place is somewhere you feel safe, relaxed, and at ease. It can be a real-life place or a place in your imagination. Thinking of your happy place and going there in your mind is a way to cope when you are feeling overwhelmed. Draw a picture of your happy place on this page. Add as many details as possible!

DATE: _____

TODAY'S MOOD: ☺ 😀 ☹ 😐 😠

Gratitude means being thankful and showing appreciation for the good things in your life. It can help you focus on positive things. Use this space to make your own gratitude list. What are you thankful for?

_____

_____

_____

_____

_____

_____

_____

_____

_____

_____

_____

_____

DATE: _____

TODAY'S MOOD: ☺ 😃 ☹ 😐 😠

What are some ways you can show thanks to other people and to your community? How can you share your gratitude with others? What are ways you can be kinder to others?

_____

_____

_____

_____

_____

_____

_____

_____

_____

_____

_____

_____

_____

_____

DATE: _____

TODAY'S MOOD:

Ten Days of Gratitude

Can you practice gratitude for ten days in a row? This list covers different things in your life. Look at the theme on each day and think about specific things that make you feel grateful. Then check it off and come back the next day!

- ☐ **Day 1:** Family and loved ones
- ☐ **Day 2:** Friends
- ☐ **Day 3:** Favorite games
- ☐ **Day 4:** School
- ☐ **Day 5:** Home and neighborhood
- ☐ **Day 6:** Pets and animals
- ☐ **Day 7:** Favorite movies and books
- ☐ **Day 8:** Learning new things
- ☐ **Day 9:** Free time to do fun things
- ☐ **Day 10:** The future

DATE: _____

TODAY'S MOOD: ☺ 😃 ☹ 😐 😠

How can you show kindness and gratitude to yourself?
Write down five ways you can show yourself love
this week.

_____

_____

_____

_____

_____

_____

_____

_____

_____

_____

_____

_____

DATE: _____

TODAY'S MOOD:

Challenge Yourself!

This activity helps you relax your muscles and your body. First, pretend you are squeezing juice out of a lemon. Squeeze your hands together as hard as you can to get all the juice out! Now drop the lemon and relax your hands. Notice how your hands feel when they are relaxed.

Next, pretend you are a kitten stretching out its front legs. Reach up your arms as high as you can and feel them pulling your shoulders. Then relax your arms down to your sides. Notice how they feel calm and relaxed.

Try it with other muscle groups, like your legs and feet. Squeeze, stretch, and release until you are relaxed all over!

DATE: _____

TODAY'S MOOD:

Heart Space

Use this page to journal your emotions for one day. Create sections in your "heart space" below with all the emotions you felt today. For emotions you feel a lot, section off more space. For emotions you only feel a little, make just a little space!

DATE: _____

TODAY'S MOOD:

A Mindful Moment

Square breathing is a technique that can help you pause and focus. All you have to do is count to four!

Take a deep breath as you count to four in your head. Then hold your breath for four counts. Slowly breathe out and—you guessed it—count to four! Finally, hold for four counts before breathing in again. Repeat as many times as you want.

Square breathing is a way of pacing your breath with specific counts. It works with your nervous system to slow your heart rate and calm your entire body.

DATE: _____

TODAY'S MOOD: 😊 😄 ☹️ 😐 😠

Everyone has trouble dealing with emotions sometimes. You are not alone! Working through difficulties is called being resilient. What are ways you can help yourself move on and move forward? What can you say to yourself to get through tough emotions? The first one has been written for you.

I will do better next time!

_____

_____

_____

_____

_____

_____

_____

_____

_____

_____

_____

DATE: _____

TODAY'S MOOD: ☺ 😀 ☹ 😐 😠

Look back at the journaling you have done in the
Heart Space section of this book. Do you think you
have a better understanding of yourself and your
emotions? What new goals might you set for yourself
at this point in your mental health journey?

_____

_____

_____

_____

_____

_____

_____

_____

_____

_____

_____

_____

_____

Express Yourself

PART 2

Head Space

Psychological mental health is your ability to understand the thoughts that go through your head. Having a healthy mind allows you to manage your negative thoughts and turn them into positive, healthy thoughts. In this section of your journal, you will learn more about your thought patterns, your goals, and your strengths!

DATE: _____

TODAY'S MOOD: 🙂 😄 🙁 😐 😠

You have lots of thoughts every single day. What are some thoughts you have that make you feel happy, excited, or good? What are thoughts that lead to a good day or a good mood?

_____

_____

_____

_____

_____

_____

_____

_____

_____

_____

_____

_____

DATE: _____

TODAY'S MOOD: ☺ 😃 😟 😐 😠

What are some thoughts that make you feel not so good? What thoughts make you feel upset, angry, worried, or scared? What are thoughts that lead to a bad day or a bad mood?

_____

_____

_____

_____

_____

_____

_____

_____

_____

_____

_____

_____

_____

_____

DATE: _____

TODAY'S MOOD: 🙂 😄 ☹️ 😐 😠

One helpful way to keep track of your thoughts is to write them all down. This helps you see how your thinking can affect your day. Start writing down your thoughts today! Think about how each thought made you feel, and describe what happened next.

Thought *I hope I don't fail my test tomorrow.*

_____

_____

_____

Feeling *Nervous*

_____

_____

_____

What happened? *I started studying more.*

_____

_____

_____

DATE: _____

TODAY'S MOOD: ☺ 😀 ☹ 😐 😠

Sometimes there are specific things or situations that lead us to have negative thoughts. They are known as "triggers." What are some of your triggers for negative thinking?

_____

_____

_____

_____

_____

_____

_____

_____

_____

_____

_____

_____

_____

DATE: _____

TODAY'S MOOD: 🙂 😃 😧 😐 😠

Do your negative thoughts have any patterns? For example, do they tend to occur in the morning, during the day at school, or at night? Do they occur on certain days of the week or around certain people? Write down any patterns you might notice.

_____

_____

_____

_____

_____

_____

_____

_____

_____

_____

_____

_____

DATE: _____

TODAY'S MOOD:

A Mindful Moment

Sometimes thoughts stick in our head. When these thoughts cause distress, it is helpful to practice mindfulness. Part of mindfulness is letting your thoughts pass in and out of your mind without judging them.

Imagine your thoughts are like clouds floating by. Allow yourself to notice each thought that comes into your head. Pay attention to the thought and accept it as a thought. Then watch it float away like a cloud. Wait for the next thought to float into your mind and do the same thing with this new thought.

Just like clouds, thoughts are neither good nor bad. They simply come and go. So practice treating your thoughts like clouds!

DATE: _____

TODAY'S MOOD: ☺ 😃 ☹ 😐 😠

Your thoughts are also very closely linked to your actions and behaviors. Write down one thought you had today. What did this thought make you feel? How did it change your emotions?

_____

_____

_____

_____

_____

_____

_____

_____

_____

_____

_____

_____

_____

_____

DATE: _____

TODAY'S MOOD: ☺ 😄 ☹ 😐 😠

Your thoughts are very closely linked to your actions and your behaviors. Write down one thought you had today. How did this thought make you act? What did this thought cause you to do?

_____

_____

_____

_____

_____

_____

_____

_____

_____

_____

_____

_____

_____

_____

DATE: _____

TODAY'S MOOD: 🙂 😀 ☹️ 😐 😠

It's time to increase your awareness of your thoughts. The more aware you are, the easier it will be to manage any emotions related to each thought. Check off any of the positive or negative thoughts you have frequently.

Negative Thoughts

☐ I'm not good enough.

☐ I'm ugly.

☐ I can't do it.

☐ Nobody likes me.

☐ I'm worthless.

Positive Thoughts

☐ I am a leader.

☐ I can do anything I put my mind to.

☐ I am in charge of my life.

☐ I can make a difference.

☐ I deserve to be loved.

DATE: _____

TODAY'S MOOD: 🙂 😀 ☹️ 😐 😠

Our thoughts, emotions, and actions are all related. We can change our unhelpful thoughts to lead to positive actions and emotions that make us feel good. How can you rewrite your unhelpful thoughts? Can you change your unhelpful thoughts so that they are more positive and supportive?

_____

_____

_____

_____

_____

_____

_____

_____

_____

_____

_____

_____

DATE: _____

TODAY'S MOOD: ☺ 😀 ☹ 😐 😠

Have you heard of self-talk? It's how you talk to yourself inside your head! How do you speak to yourself in a kind and compassionate way? For example, you may say, "I was a great friend to Natasha today."

_____

_____

_____

_____

_____

_____

_____

_____

_____

_____

_____

_____

_____

DATE: _____

TODAY'S MOOD: ☺ 😀 ☹ 😐 😠

Negative self-talk is when you are hard on yourself or put yourself down. What are some examples of negative self-talk? How do you speak to yourself in a judgmental or unsupportive way?

_____

_____

_____

_____

_____

_____

_____

_____

_____

_____

_____

_____

_____

_____

DATE: _____

TODAY'S MOOD:

A Mindful Moment

Affirmations are positive statements that you say to yourself. You can say them in your head or aloud. Positive affirmations make you feel empowered! They can help you reach goals, build confidence, and improve your physical and mental health.

Repeating affirmations every day helps your brain realize that they are true. It also helps your brain feel ready to take on the day. Affirmations help you stay mindful and think positively.

Here are some examples of positive affirmations. Fill the rest of the page with your own affirmations.

I am smart.

I am powerful.

I love myself.

_____

_____

_____

DATE: _____

TODAY'S MOOD: 🙂 😀 😧 😐 😠

Negative self-talk can be hurtful and harmful! Can you think of ways to change the negative things you say to yourself? How can you transform your negative self-talk into positive self-talk?

_____

_____

_____

_____

_____

_____

_____

_____

_____

_____

_____

_____

_____

_____

DATE: _____

TODAY'S MOOD: ☺ 😀 ☹ 😐 😠

What has been your favorite prompt or activity in the
Head Space section of this book? Do you feel more
connected with your thoughts? What are you hoping
to learn next?

_____

_____

_____

_____

_____

_____

_____

_____

_____

_____

_____

_____

_____

DATE: _____

TODAY'S MOOD: ☺ 😄 ☹ 😐 😠

Self-confidence is trust in yourself and your abilities. It makes you feel strong, powerful, and capable! What does self-confidence mean to you? What makes you feel confident? What are things you say to yourself to boost your confidence?

_____

_____

_____

_____

_____

_____

_____

_____

_____

_____

_____

_____

_____

_____

DATE: _____

TODAY'S MOOD: ☺ 😃 ☹ 😐 😠

Your self-esteem is related to your confidence. When you have a healthy self-esteem, you feel happy with who you are. How would you describe your current level of self-esteem? What are things you do well? What are things you like about yourself?

_____

_____

_____

_____

_____

_____

_____

_____

_____

_____

_____

_____

_____

DATE: _____

TODAY'S MOOD:

Challenge Yourself!

One of the best ways to build up your self-esteem is by doing things you are great at! These activities could include playing an instrument, working on computer code, playing with your friends, doing chores, or playing a sport. For this challenge, do an activity that makes you feel happy and proud. Be sure to focus on how that activity makes you feel and think!

DATE: _____

TODAY'S MOOD: 🙂 😄 😧 😐 😠

Sometimes life is really hard. When was a time in your life when things were tough? What did you do to get through it? What skills did you use to keep going?

_____

_____

_____

_____

_____

_____

_____

_____

_____

_____

_____

_____

_____

DATE: _____

TODAY'S MOOD:

A Mindful Moment

A growth mindset is when you are open to learning, growing, and changing over time. It means you believe that your skills will improve through hard work.

The opposite of growth mindset is "fixed mindset." A fixed mindset is believing you will be the same forever and cannot change. One way to challenge a fixed mindset is by meditating. Read the script below to build your growth mindset.

Imagine you are standing on top of a mountain. In front of you is the entire world at your fingertips. Focus on your breathing. Take a deep breath in and a deep breath out. Say the following statements aloud to yourself:

I believe I can change. I believe my skills and talents will grow stronger with practice. Hard work will help me accomplish my goals. I see my failures as a chance to learn. When people give me feedback, I view it as a guide to help me improve.

Now close your eyes and try it yourself!

DATE: _____

TODAY'S MOOD: 🙂 😃 😧 😐 😠

What are some lessons you have learned from past mistakes? If you could write a letter to encourage your future self to keep going and keep working hard, what would it say?

_____

_____

_____

_____

_____

_____

_____

_____

_____

_____

_____

_____

_____

DATE: _____

TODAY'S MOOD: ☺ 😃 ☹ 😐 😠

Do you find yourself needing things to be perfect all the time? This is called perfectionism. When do you find yourself being a perfectionist? How does perfectionism get in your way?

_____

_____

_____

_____

_____

_____

_____

_____

_____

_____

_____

_____

_____

_____

_____

DATE: _____

TODAY'S MOOD: ☺ 😀 ☹ 😐 😠

When you start to worry about things you cannot control, try to think about what you *can* control. Over the next few days, put a check mark next to anything you find yourself worrying about.

Things I Can Control

☐ My own emotions

☐ My own thoughts

☐ My actions and behaviors

☐ The way I react to situations

☐ My attitude

☐ My words or what I say

Things I Cannot Control

☐ What other people think

☐ What other people say

☐ How other people feel

☐ What happens in the world around me

☐ Other people's decisions

☐ The past or things that have already happened

DATE: _____

TODAY'S MOOD: 😊 😃 🙁 😐 😠

We all have goals and things that we want to do in our lives. What are your short-term goals? These are goals you want to achieve in the next few days, weeks, or months.

_____

_____

_____

_____

_____

_____

_____

_____

_____

_____

_____

_____

_____

DATE: _____

TODAY'S MOOD:

A Mindful Moment

One way to focus your mind is by using your five senses: sight, sound, smell, taste, and touch. Doing so can help you slow down and stay in the present moment.

Take a deep breath, look around, and check in with each of your senses. Start with sight. What are the first five things you see? Then try to find four things you feel with your hands, feet, or other parts of your body. Finally, notice three things you hear, two things you smell, and one thing you taste.

The best thing about this activity is that you can do it anywhere you go! By taking in the world around you, you can stay grounded and stay mindful.

Five things you can see

1. _____

2. _____

3. _____

4. _____

5. _____

Four things you can feel

1. _____

2. _____

3. _____

4. _____

Three things you can hear

1. _____

2. _____

3. _____

Two things you can smell

1. _____

2. _____

One thing you can taste

1. _____

DATE: _____

TODAY'S MOOD: ☺ 😃 ☹ 😐 😠

What are your passions? What are things in your
life that you love doing or thinking about? What is
something you could talk about for hours and not
get bored? What is a topic you would love to learn
more about?

_____

_____

_____

_____

_____

_____

_____

_____

_____

_____

_____

_____

_____

_____

DATE: _____

TODAY'S MOOD: ☺ 😀 ☹ 😐 😠

Look back at the journaling you have done in the
Head Space section of this book. Do you think you
have a better understanding of yourself and your
thoughts? What new goals might you set for yourself
at this point in your mental health journey?

_____

_____

_____

_____

_____

_____

_____

_____

_____

_____

_____

_____

_____

_____

Express Yourself

PART 3

Shared Space

Social mental health is how you relate to other people. Humans are naturally social creatures, which means we crave attention and interaction with others! This section will help you navigate the social world by exploring how you create relationships and friendships.

DATE: _____

TODAY'S MOOD: 🙂 😄 ☹️ 😐 😠

What does it mean to be a good friend? What traits or qualities do you look for in your friends?

_____

_____

_____

_____

_____

_____

_____

_____

_____

_____

_____

_____

_____

_____

_____

DATE: _____

TODAY'S MOOD: ☺ 😃 ☹ 😐 😠

When you make a new friend, it's fun to learn more about them. What questions could you ask them? What do you want to learn about your new friend?

_____

_____

_____

_____

_____

_____

_____

_____

_____

_____

_____

_____

_____

_____

_____

DATE: _____

TODAY'S MOOD:

Challenge Yourself!

One great way to make friends is by giving compliments! A compliment is a statement that is kind and nice. For example, "I like your shirt" or "You are a really funny person!" are friendly things you can say to someone. Your challenge is to go out and give as many friendly compliments as you can for the rest of the day. Notice how people react when you compliment them, and notice how it makes you feel happy, too!

DATE: _____

TODAY'S MOOD: 🙂 😃 🙁 😐 😠

Being left out is no fun. Part of being a good friend is including other people. What are ways you can try to include everyone in games and playtime? How can you invite in someone who feels left out?

_____

_____

_____

_____

_____

_____

_____

_____

_____

_____

_____

_____

_____

DATE: _____

TODAY'S MOOD: 😊 😄 😧 😐 😠

Have you ever felt nervous in public? Have you ever been afraid to speak up in a group? It's normal to feel shy when you first meet people! Use this page to think about skills and strategies to help you open up when you feel shy.

_____

_____

_____

_____

_____

_____

_____

_____

_____

_____

_____

_____

_____

A Mindful Moment

If you start to feel nervous or anxious in public, a body scan can often help you calm down. This technique lets you check in with different parts of your body. It's okay to stop this exercise if you feel uncomfortable or if it brings up negative feelings.

Take a slow, deep breath. As you breathe out, bring your attention to your body. First, focus on your head and your face. What do you feel? Blink your eyes and scrunch up your nose. What do you notice?

Now focus on your arms. Clench your fists and let them go. Raise your shoulders up to your ears, and then drop them back down. What do you feel in your arms?

Now focus on your torso, the middle part of your body. Move your stomach in and out. Feel your ribs as you breathe in and out. What do you notice?

Finally, focus on your legs and your feet. Curl your toes. Bend your knees back and forth. What do you feel? Take one final deep breath in and out.

DATE: _____

TODAY'S MOOD: ☺ 😀 ☹ 😐 😠

One way to be a good friend is to encourage your friends to do their best! How can you help those around you be the best that they can be? How can you be encouraging to others?

_____

_____

_____

_____

_____

_____

_____

_____

_____

_____

_____

_____

_____

_____

_____

DATE: _____

TODAY'S MOOD: 🙂 😀 🙁 😐 😣

Part of being a good friend is being your best possible self! How can you be your best self with your friends? What are your biggest strengths that you can show to other people? What do other people most love about you?

_____

_____

_____

_____

_____

_____

_____

_____

_____

_____

_____

_____

_____

_____

DATE: _____

TODAY'S MOOD: 🙂 😄 ☹️ 😐 😠

Knowing your strengths helps you be your best self with friends, family, and everyone around you. Look at this list of common words we use to describe people. Check off the traits that you think you have. Can you use them to be a good friend and a good person in public? Use the blank lines to write in other traits you love about yourself!

- ☐ Friendly
- ☐ Helpful
- ☐ Serious
- ☐ Smart
- ☐ Relaxed
- ☐ _____
- ☐ _____
- ☐ _____

- ☐ Kind
- ☐ Funny
- ☐ Loving
- ☐ Trustworthy
- ☐ Responsible
- ☐ _____
- ☐ _____
- ☐ _____

DATE: _____

TODAY'S MOOD: ☺ 😄 ☹ 😐 😠

What does respect mean to you? How do you show respect to others? What does being respectful look like at home, at school, and with friends?

_____

_____

_____

_____

_____

_____

_____

_____

_____

_____

_____

_____

_____

_____

_____

_____

DATE: _____

TODAY'S MOOD:

A Mindful Moment

Mindfulness is all about being in the present moment. One way to be present is through coloring! This soothing activity allows you to focus on lines, patterns, shapes, colors, and design. Try coloring this picture to simply focus on the present moment.

DATE: _____

TODAY'S MOOD: ☺ 😀 ☹ 😐 😠

Being helpful is a great way to interact with other people. What ways can you be helpful today? How can you be helpful at home, at school, and with your friends?

_____

_____

_____

_____

_____

_____

_____

_____

_____

_____

_____

_____

_____

DATE: _____

TODAY'S MOOD: ☺ 😃 ☹ 😐 😠

What has been your favorite prompt or activity in the Shared Space section of this book? Do you feel more connected with your thoughts? What are you hoping to learn next?

_____

_____

_____

_____

_____

_____

_____

_____

_____

_____

_____

_____

DATE: _____

TODAY'S MOOD: ☺ 😄 ☹ 😐 😠

Do you know what empathy is? Empathy is understanding how other people feel and showing kindness and compassion to them. When is a time you felt empathy for someone else?

_____

_____

_____

_____

_____

_____

_____

_____

_____

_____

_____

_____

_____

DATE: _____

TODAY'S MOOD: ☺ 😀 ☹ 😐 😠

Empathy lets you understand a situation from someone else's perspective. When was the last time you had an argument with someone? Could you have seen the situation from their point of view?

_____

_____

_____

_____

_____

_____

_____

_____

_____

_____

_____

_____

_____

DATE: _____

TODAY'S MOOD: 😊 😃 ☹️ 😐 😠

What do you do when you see someone having a
hard time or struggling with something? How can you
help comfort them?

_____

_____

_____

_____

_____

_____

_____

_____

_____

_____

_____

_____

_____

_____

_____

_____

DATE: _____

TODAY'S MOOD:

You can show kindness to others by giving them your attention and listening to them. Have you ever heard of active listening? It's when you simply listen to another person, ask them questions, respond to them with kindness, and try not to judge them. Active listening is a great way to practice your empathy skills! Read through these tips on how to be a mindful active listener.

1. Look the other person in the eyes.

2. Keep your ears open only to them, focusing closely on what they say.

3. Nod to show you are listening.

4. Do not judge the other person. Just remain neutral and calm.

5. Ask them questions to get more information.

6. Think about how the person might be feeling.

7. Respond with kindness and empathy.

DATE: _____

TODAY'S MOOD: ☺ 😃 ☹ 😐 😠

Conflict, whether it's small or big, will happen in life. How do you deal with conflict with your friends and family? How do you make your opinions known? What strategies seem to work best for you?

_____

_____

_____

_____

_____

_____

_____

_____

_____

_____

_____

_____

_____

_____

DATE: _____

TODAY'S MOOD:

Challenge Yourself!

Next time you have a conflict with someone, try these simple steps to help you both get through it!

1. Pause to stay calm and focused on the situation.

2. What do you feel? What does the other person feel?

3. What are you thinking? What is the other person thinking?

4. Try to understand the other person's perspective and see the situation from their side.

5. Take action. Try apologizing, problem-solving, walking away, or compromising.

6. Follow up with the person later to see how they are doing and if the solution is still working.

DATE: _____

TODAY'S MOOD: ☺ 😀 ☹ 😐 😣

It can be hard to ask for help, but asking for help is a sign of strength! Think of a recent situation where you wanted to ask for help but didn't. What could you have done or said? How could you have reached out? Who could you have reached out to?

_____

_____

_____

_____

_____

_____

_____

_____

_____

_____

_____

_____

_____

DATE: _____

TODAY'S MOOD: 🙂 😄 ☹️ 😐 😠

Receiving feedback can often be hard. It might make you feel uncomfortable, even though it is meant to be helpful! What are ways you can help yourself accept feedback? How can you use feedback to create new goals for yourself? How can you use feedback to try harder next time?

_____

_____

_____

_____

_____

_____

_____

_____

_____

_____

_____

_____

DATE: _____

TODAY'S MOOD:

Comparing yourself to others can cause you to feel bad about yourself. Remember, we are all different. The things that make us unique are wonderful! How can you appreciate the strengths of others and your own strengths at the same time?

_____

_____

_____

_____

_____

_____

_____

_____

_____

_____

_____

_____

_____

_____

DATE: _____

TODAY'S MOOD: ☺ 😃 ☹ 😐 😠

Comparing yourself to others can sometimes lead to negative thoughts. Use this list as a reminder of all the good things about yourself!

One thing I am really good at doing:

1. _____

Two things I might want to be when I grow up:

1. _____

2. _____

Three positive words that describe me:

1. _____

2. _____

3. _____

Four things I like doing:

1. _____ 3. _____

2. _____ 4. _____

Five things I am proud of:

1. _____ 4. _____

2. _____ 5. _____

3. _____

DATE: _____

TODAY'S MOOD: 🙂 😀 😧 😐 😠

An extrovert is someone who gets an energy boost when they are around other people. When do you feel energized by being around other people?

_____

_____

_____

_____

_____

_____

_____

_____

_____

_____

_____

_____

_____

_____

DATE: _____

TODAY'S MOOD: ☺ 😄 ☹ 😐 😠

An introvert is someone who feels recharged when they spend some time alone. When do you feel more like an introvert? When are times you would prefer some space just for you?

_____

_____

_____

_____

_____

_____

_____

_____

_____

_____

_____

_____

A Mindful Moment

Yoga is a great way to stay mindful. Try this Tadasana pose to feel open and energized.

Stand up straight and tall like a mountain. Keep your hands at your sides. Take a deep breath through your nose and a long breath out of your mouth.

Now it's time to cool off and calm down. The Shavasana pose will help you relax and feel grounded. Lie on your back with your arms by your sides and your feet relaxed. Take deep breaths in through your nose and out through your mouth.

DATE: _____

TODAY'S MOOD: ☺ 😃 ☹ 😐 😠

Being social is important, but having alone time is important, too. It is all about balance! How can you find a good balance between your personal time and your social time? When do you notice yourself craving social interaction? When do you notice yourself craving quiet time to yourself?

_____

_____

_____

_____

_____

_____

_____

_____

_____

_____

DATE: _____

TODAY'S MOOD: 🙂 😃 😧 😐 😣

Look back at the journaling you have done in the
Shared Space section of this book. Do you think you
have a better understanding of yourself and your
thoughts? What new goals might you set for yourself
at this point in your mental health journey?

_____

_____

_____

_____

_____

_____

_____

_____

_____

_____

_____

_____

_____

_____

Express Yourself

RESOURCES

BOOKS

CBT Workbook for Kids by Dr. Heather Davidson

Empathy Workbook for Kids by Dr. Hiedi France

Mindfulness Workbook for Kids by Hannah Sherman

APPS

(Be sure to ask your parent or guardian for permission before downloading any apps.)

Kids To-Do List

This app helps you keep track of everything in your life. Once you create your list, you can start checking off all the items!

Smiling Mind

This app helps increase your mindfulness skills! It helps with daily stressors and gives you positive solutions for times when you feel overwhelmed.

Acknowledgments

I am so grateful for everyone who has helped me in the process of creating this mental health journal. First, to my parents, who have supported me every step of my journey and who have always believed that I would succeed. Second, my husband, who is one of my fiercest supporters through thick and thin. Third, to Callisto, for giving me this opportunity, and to my editor, Barbara, for making this process fun. And finally, to all my clients and their families, for helping shape me as a clinician and for reminding me how much resilience exists in this world.

About the Author

 **Becca Heiden, PhD** is a licensed clinical psychologist currently working as a staff psychologist at the Children's Hospital of Philadelphia Center for ADHD Management. She is passionate about working with children, teens, and families through both psychological assessment and therapy services. Dr. Heiden received her bachelor's degree in psychology from the University of Notre Dame and her master's and doctoral degrees from Miami University. She completed her dissertation on social emotional learning in school-age children. Dr. Heiden lives in Philadelphia, Pennsylvania with her husband, Brendan, and their cat, Barlow.

CPSIA information can be obtained
at www.ICGtesting.com
Printed in the USA
JSHW021959021022
31158JS00003B/8

9 781685 397210